Changing Land

Written by Liz Miles

Contents

Collins

Stanley Primary School

Introduction

Land is always changing shape. The way people use the land changes over time, and this, in turn, changes the look of the land. Like detectives, we can search for clues in any town or part of the countryside to discover what has changed, and why.

Several docks, like Seaforth Dock near Liverpool, were built along the River Mersey, so that ships can stop to load and unload their cargo.

new houses in Bury St Edmunds, Suffolk

The way people use the land depends on natural features like mountains, rivers and coastlines. For example, people can't grow food on a rocky mountain, but they might be able to use it for skiing or climbing.

As people's needs change, the way they use the land changes too. A growing **population** needs more homes, so farmland once used for growing food or grazing animals might be used to build new houses.

Land use – town and country

Land use in towns and cities (urban areas) and the countryside (rural areas) changes in different ways and at different speeds.

Skye

Portree

Portree: the main town on the Isle of Skye, a mountainous island connected to the Scottish mainland by a bridge. Only about 2,500 people live in Portree.

In this book, we'll explore the large English town of Colchester, Essex. We'll also look at the Scottish Isle of Skye, in the Inner Hebrides, and its biggest town – Portree. We'll find clues that show why land use has changed a lot in Colchester over time, and why many changes have happened quite fast. On Skye, we'll see that changes have happened more slowly.

Colchester: one of the UK's oldest towns. The ancient Romans who invaded Britain nearly 2,000 years ago built their capital city here. About 180,000 people live in Colchester today.

Colchester

Colchester – past and present

A map of Colchester helps us to see how the land was used at the time when the map was drawn. Spotting the differences between past and present maps shows some big changes, such as new industries and transport. We can also see changes in the way people have used natural features, such as rivers.

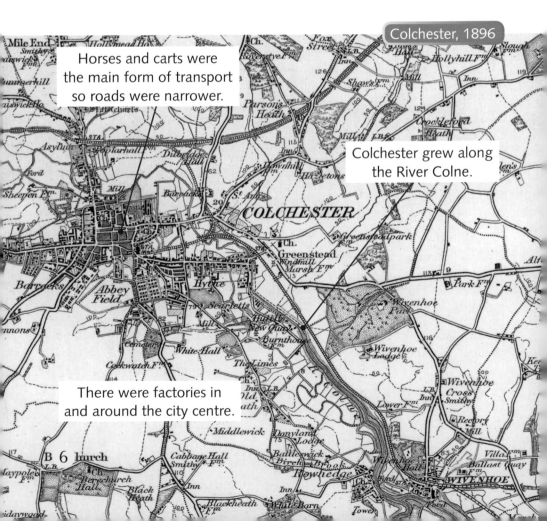

Colchester, 1896

Horses and carts were the main form of transport so roads were narrower.

Colchester grew along the River Colne.

There were factories in and around the city centre.

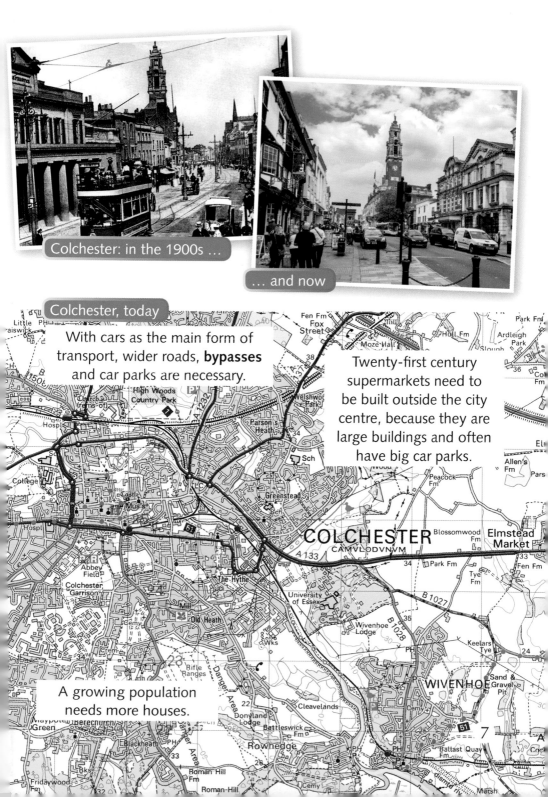

Colchester: in the 1900s ...

... and now

Colchester, today

With cars as the main form of transport, wider roads, **bypasses** and car parks are necessary.

Twenty-first century supermarkets need to be built outside the city centre, because they are large buildings and often have big car parks.

A growing population needs more houses.

Underground

Underground clues show how some of the first people to live in the Colchester area used the land. **Archaeologists** have discovered ditches dug into the earth, coins and other clues showing there was a big **settlement** here over 2,000 years ago. People used ditches and two rivers to protect the settlement from attack.

The ancient Romans invaded and turned the settlement into a wealthy Roman town.

We know there was a Roman town at Colchester because archaeologists have found the remains of Roman buildings such as houses, a chariot-racing arena, a theatre and temples.

archaeologists at the site of Colchester's Roman chariot-racing arena

Some evidence of the Romans is above ground too. These are the remains of a gate in the wall that surrounded the Roman town.

Boudica

Much of Colchester had to be rebuilt after Boudica, queen of a local tribe, led a rebellion against the Romans in about 60 CE and destroyed most of the buildings.

Castles and mills

Land use changed again in the years after the Romans left in the 5th century. Tribes called Anglo-Saxons moved in, building their own wooden hut-like homes on top of the empty, fallen-down Roman buildings.

Colchester became important again after 1066, when the Normans from France, led by William the Conqueror, took control of England. Because of its location, the Normans built a castle in Colchester to help defend the east of England.

By the 1300s, Colchester was a busy market town where many people made and sold cloth. A small port was built on the River Colne where ships could load up with cloth and take it to be sold overseas.

The Norman castle **keep** was built on the foundations of a Roman temple.

Water-powered mills were used to make cloth from sheep's wool.

Clues from maps

In this map from the 1600s, the streets still follow the lines of the old Roman streets.

Homes

By examining the oldest houses in Colchester, we can find clues as to what was happening when they were built.

Dutch-speaking weavers and cloth makers from Flanders (present-day Belgium) once lived in the "Dutch Quarter". In the 1570s, they had to flee from Flanders because they were being persecuted for their religious beliefs. In the Dutch Quarter, the houses' big windows let in lots of light, so the weavers could see as they made cloth on their looms.

In the late 1800s, nearly 300 new houses were built in an area called New Town. They were needed for more workers and managers, as new industries developed and factories were built, like Paxman's who made diesel engines.

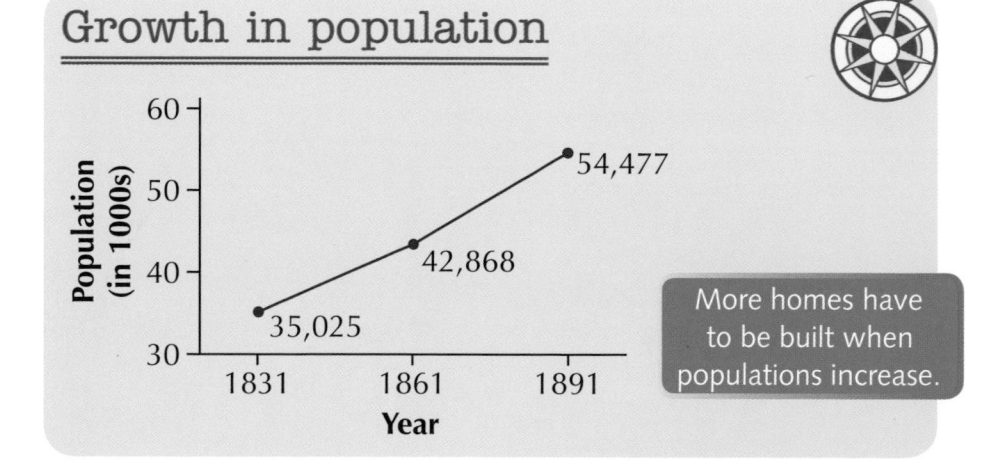

Growth in population

Population (in 1000s)

60
50 — 54,477
40 — 42,868
30 — 35,025

1831   1861   1891
Year

More homes have to be built when populations increase.

The long window is called a "weaver's window".

Terraces of houses in New Town were home to workers in the engineering and clothing industries.

New industries

After 1880, big factories were built, where new machinery was used to make clothes, boots and shoes. A new engineering industry with more modern machinery made boilers, engines and farm equipment.

With a growing population, changing needs and new inventions, Colchester changed too, and most of the town centre factories were knocked down in the 21st century. Shops, banks, restaurants and offices – known as service industries – took the place of factories and workshops.

From offices to shops

We can spot clues of changes in old buildings. Lettering above the shops on this high street building shows it was the offices for the fire-fighting department. It was built in 1820.

workers at a Victorian factory, where metal goods were made

Ships and quays

Different needs have changed land use along the River Colne, as we can see from illustrations and photographs of Colchester's small port, the Hythe.

Quays were built at the Hythe from the 14th century onwards so that ships could bring goods like soap, spices and silk into Colchester. Ships took other goods made in Colchester, such as cloth, along the river to the sea, for sale in other countries.

This picture from 1808 shows workers loading goods on to barges.

Colchester oyster fishermen at work, 1952

The river is narrow and winding, so only small ships and boats could easily reach the port from the sea. As the river has **silted** up, and railways and roads are used more and more to carry goods, the way the Hythe is used has changed completely. The quays are used for riverside homes, including accommodation for students studying at the nearby Essex University.

University of Essex accommodation blocks at Hythe Quay

Roads, rails and bridges

The population of the Colchester area nearly doubled between 1945 and 2000. More people began to live in and around Colchester and work in London, as faster trains and wider roads made it possible to travel quickly between the two places.

As the population expanded, thousands more houses were built on land further out from the town centre. Traffic jams led to the building of a bypass in 1933. Ring roads with roundabouts were designed to keep traffic out of the town centre.

A modern sculpture of Boudica stands on a roundabout in the midst of traffic near Colchester's main railway station.

the Tollgate Centre Retail Park, in the **suburbs** of Colchester

Many shops, companies and offices moved out of town to retail parks or industrial estates, where shoppers find parking easier.

Colchester – the evidence

Colchester's location has made it popular for increasing numbers of people since Roman times. Land use reflects changing needs, from Norman castle fortifications to modern supermarkets.

Although change has been dramatic, with entire areas being flattened and replaced with new buildings, roads and factories, plenty of evidence of past land use still exists. The evidence is found in the town centre streets, Roman and other ruins, photographs and pictures, and old maps.

Old photos like this of Colchester High Street in 1952 show businesses that are now gone, and others, like the hotel, that still exist.

Old engravings of Colchester from books, like this from 1779, give us a clue about the importance of the river and the size of the town.

What's in a name?

Road names are clues to land use of the past. The old road name, Cornhill, reminds us how important corn used to be for Colchester in medieval times. There used to be a corn market here.

HIGH STREET
FORMERLY CORNHILL

Isle of Skye – past and present

The Isle of Skye is 764 kilometres from Colchester. It's the largest of a group of islands off the west coast of Scotland. It's harder to spot differences in maps of Skye from the past and present. Because Skye is a long way from big towns, and it has high mountains and a rugged coastline, the changes in land use have been slower. Unlike Colchester's ever-growing population, Skye's population got smaller for many years.

Isle of Skye, 1832

No roads can pass over the mountains.

Houses are sparse.

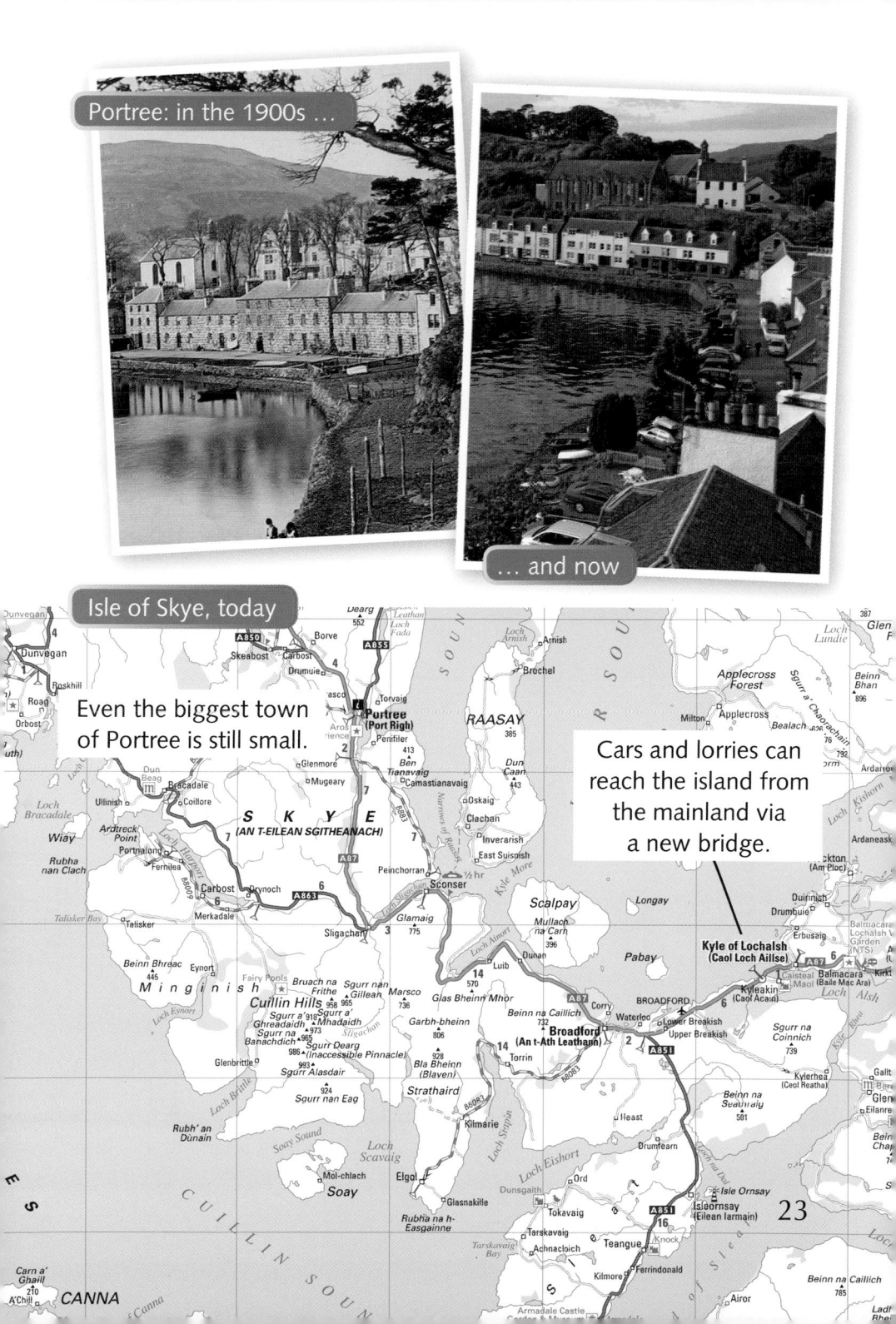

Portree: in the 1900s …

… and now

Isle of Skye, today

Even the biggest town of Portree is still small.

Cars and lorries can reach the island from the mainland via a new bridge.

23

Rocks and forts

In around 6000 BCE, the earliest people on Skye used stones to make tools, and built monuments out of rocks. We think that they ate shellfish because big piles of shells have been found. Ancient tunnels and forts have been found too.

From medieval times, land was used for castles too, like Dunvegan Castle, which is set out on a rock overlooking the sea. Generations of the MacLeod **clan** have lived there for more than 750 years.

Around 2,300 years ago, stone was used to build forts called "brochs", high up on hills for a good view.

The MacLeods built Dunvegan Castle on top of an older fort in about 1350.

Moving on

In the past, lots of the islanders grew food on small bits of land, and kept a few sheep. These people, called "crofters", paid **rent** to the clan chiefs who were the landowners.

Crofters stayed in shelters, called "sheilings", to look after their sheep in the hills.

The landowners made money from the crofters' rent and from seaweed gathered from the shores, which was sold to make soap and fertilisers. But later, they found more money could be made from sheep's wool. So in the 1700s and early 1800s, the landowners cleared the crofters away and used the land to graze sheep. Many people were forced to leave the island on ships in search of a new life abroad. Some of the crofters' ruined houses can still be seen today.

The fallen-down houses of Boreraig remind us that a whole village of people was forced to leave.

Empty spaces

The mountains and **lochs** on Skye mean only about a tenth of the land can be used for farming. Most of the farms **rear** sheep.

For thousands of years, the only way of getting on and off the island was by boat. Skye's rocky coastline has few places where harbours can be built or boats can land safely.

The bay at Portree was wide enough to build a harbour. Portree is the largest town on the island.

The coastline of Skye has lots of cliffs and narrow sea inlets.

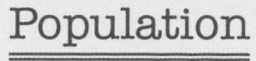

Population

The population of Skye got smaller between the 1840s and the 1990s because:

- there were fewer opportunities for crofters
- there were few other jobs available on Skye
- there were fewer services, such as hospitals and leisure facilities like cinemas, than on the mainland
- it took a long time to travel to the mainland.

The Gaelic language was still spoken by most people on Skye until the 1920s.

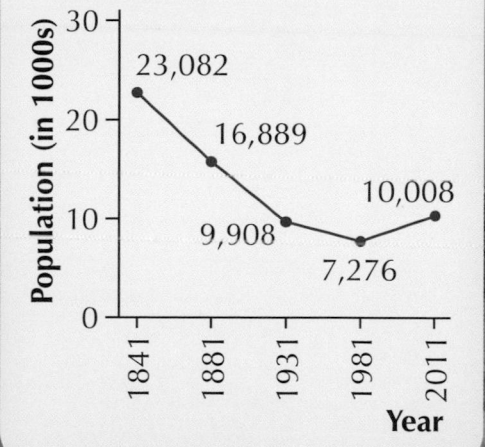

Networks

A bridge connecting Skye with the mainland was opened in 1995. Instead of queuing for ferries, residents, visitors and lorries could drive over the bridge. Skye's roads were improved and a faster broadband internet service was set up in 2012, so the island was better connected to the rest of the world.

Tourists use the wild landscape for walks and to explore nature.

the Skye Bridge

The wind drives turbines to make electricity.

Around this time, more people started to live on the island. There were new buildings for homes, businesses and tourists. Land has also been used for wind turbines as a new source of power.

Isle of Skye –
the evidence

From photos and maps, we can see how slowly changes in land use happened. However, two events did speed things up: the landowners forcing the crofters to leave, and the building of the bridge.

Quiet harbours

Another coastal town, Uig, has changed little since its harbour was built in the 1840s. Originally, people got on steamships from the pier to go to other  islands, but today they drive cars on to ferries.

Some old crofters' cottages are now holiday homes for tourists.

Large areas, such as the mountains, haven't changed since the earliest settlers. Little of the coast has changed, except for coves like Portree where the harbour was built in the 1800s.

New growth

Skye's population got smaller until the 1980s. Since then, new industries have appeared, such as tourism, and the population has continued to increase.

Comparing Colchester...

By gathering evidence in Colchester and Skye, we can compare land-use changes.

LION WALK MOSAIC

A COPY OF PART OF A 4TH-CENTURY ROMAN MOSAIC, FOUND IN 1976. THE PAVEMENT WOULD HAVE BEEN SQUARE WITH A CENTRAL PANEL AND FOUR SEMI-CIRCULAR ONES AROUND THE SIDES OF WHICH THIS IS ONE. THE MOSAIC LAY UNDERNEATH LION WALK. THE MEDIEVAL LANE WHICH EXTENDED SOUTHWARDS FROM THE REAR OF RED LION YARD. LION WALK WAS ORIGINALLY KNOWN AS CAT LANE, SO THE PRESENCE UNDER THE STREET OF A ROMAN MOSAIC SHOWING A WALKING LION IS A COINCIDENCE.

A copy of a 4th-century Roman mosaic. The original was discovered under the pavement of what is now a modern shopping arcade.

This narrow entrance to the Red Lion Hotel in Colchester was built for horse-led carriages. It's now a walkway to Lion Walk, a shopping arcade.

Colchester's old football stadium held 6,320 spectators. The new Colchester Community Stadium (shown here) was built further out of town in 2008 to fit over 10,000 spectators.

...and Skye

Tourism is an important industry today. A museum has rebuilt a group of cottages to show how crofters lived and worked.

Ruined castles, like Castle Moil, used to be the homes of powerful clans who battled against each other.

On Skye, you can find ancient standing stones like these on remote hilltops.

35

What do YOU think?

Why do you think the changes in land use have been so different in Colchester and on Skye?

More people came to live in Colchester, so they needed more homes and the suburbs grew fast.

The population of Skye went down through history so there was less need for new homes.

Lots of new roads were built around Colchester to avoid traffic jams.

Colchester's industries changed land use – factories had to be built for new industries like manufacturing, and then they were knocked down as offices and retail parks became more important.

Skye didn't have big factories. Farming and fishing were the main industries.

The Skye Bridge was the most important new road for the island because it made it easier to get to and from the mainland.

The future

Land use continues to change in Colchester and Skye. Sometimes, changes in land use can cause problems such as pollution and extra traffic. Town planners need to think about how to reduce these problems.

Crofting, the traditional way of farming on Skye, is being supported by charities like the **RSPB** because they help preserve a landscape where rare creatures like corncrakes and great yellow bumblebees live.

Bird watchers visit Skye to see rare species like this corncrake.

Requests to expand fish farms in the lochs on Skye have been refused because planners are worried that the farms will affect local wildlife and cause pollution.

Mussels, a popular shellfish, are grown on Skye using environmentally friendly methods.

As more retail parks were built around Colchester, fewer people went into the town centre. Planners tried to entice them back. For example, when the old bus station was moved, a large new art gallery was built costing £25 million. The bus station waiting room was transformed into a lively café. Funds were raised to change an old police station into a centre for new creative businesses.

Firstsite, the Colchester art gallery, opened in 2011.

Your locality

You can be a detective and find out how land use has changed in your area!

Look at the land around you. Features like hills, forests, rivers and coasts can have an effect on the way land is used.

For instance, if you live by the sea, some of the land might be used for tourist attractions such as funfairs or piers.

Or there may be areas where there are no buildings because of the danger of flooding by the sea.

Places like Dawlish in Devon are at risk from flooding by the sea during stormy weather. They need special flood defences to keep out the water.

The town of Great Malvern has grown up below the steep hills.

Places a long way from the sea can also be changed by
the shape of the land around them. The town of Great Malvern
lies just under the Malvern Hills. The hills have affected
the shape of the town, and have also brought lots of tourists
who enjoy walking and exploring.

Clues in buildings

You can find lots of clues in buildings in your city, town or village. Look for old buildings that are used in modern ways, such as warehouses that have been changed into flats.

Old warehouses like these have been converted into modern flats in London.

Find out the history of old buildings through books or the internet. Imagine what stories the changing land of your town or village might tell!

This old fire station is now a cafe.

Glossary

archaeologists scientists who examine old objects and places to find out about life in the past

bypasses roads that go around the outside of a city or town centre

clan family

keep tower

lochs Scottish word for lakes

population the total number of people living in an area, such as in a town, island or country

quays places built alongside the river or sea where boats and ships can stop

rear to look after animals and make sure more animals are born, usually on a farm

rent money paid to a landowner in exchange for living and farming on their land

RSPB Royal Society for the Protection of Birds

settlement a place where people live; it can be any size, from a single house to a huge city

silted when a river has filled up with sandy mud, making it narrower and shallower

suburbs areas of land where people live, which are just outside the centre of a town or city

Index

Land detective's scrapbook

Colchester and Portree are different in lots of ways!

Colchester

Housing
Lots of houses were built as Colchester's population grew.

Transport
Big towns like Colchester need big roads, roundabouts and bypasses.

Changes in building use
Lots of old buildings in Colchester are now used for different things.

Portree

Housing
Portree's population stayed small for a long time, so fewer houses were built.

Transport
The Skye Bridge opened in 1995 and made it much easier to get between Skye and the mainland.

Changes in building use
These old cottages near Portree are now holiday homes.

Ideas for reading

Written by Clare Dowdall, PhD
Lecturer and Primary Literacy Consultant

Reading objectives:
- retrieve and record information from non-fiction
- read books that are structured in different ways
- discuss their understanding and explain the meaning of words in context
- make predictions from details stated and implied

Spoken language objectives:
- use spoken language to develop understanding through speculating, hypothesising, imagining and exploring ideas
- participate in discussions, presentations, performances, role play, improvisations and debates

Curriculum links: Geography – land use; History – local history study

Resources: Local maps and photographs, ICT

Build a context for reading
- Explain that you will be reading about changing landscapes. Ask children if and how their local landscape has changed.
- Look at the cover and read the blurb. Ask children what they notice about the images on the front cover i.e. same place but at different times.
- List children's ideas about how land might change over time (elicit ideas about natural and human changes).

Understand and apply reading strategies
- Look at the contents together and discuss how the book is organised (introduction, Colchester, Isle of Skye, comparison, the future).
- Look closely at the photographs of Seaforth Dock and Bury St Edmunds. Practise being land change detectives and discuss the changes that the children can spot.